The
ENTREPRENEURIAL
LAWYER

The
ENTREPRENEURIAL
LAWYER

A Guide to Creating a Thriving
Law Firm and a Satisfying Life

Written by the founders of The American Academy of Estate
Planning Attorneys and co-authors of *The E-Myth Attorney*

ROBERT ARMSTRONG and SANFORD M. FISCH

Eleven Essential Systems: A Guide to Creating a
Thriving Law Firm and a Satisfying Life

ISBN-13: 978-1534703292

ISBN-10: 1534703292

Printed in the United States of America

Cover and interior design: Adina Cucicov, Flamingo Designs

Introduction

SYSTEM 1

SYSTEM 2

SYSTEM 3

SYSTEM 4

SYSTEM 5

SYSTEM 6

SYSTEM 7

SYSTEM 8

PLANNING AND BENCHMARKS

Running a successful law practice means wearing two hats. Your clients are counting on you to be an expert in your area of law. At the same time, you have all the demands of running a small business—something many of us didn't fully anticipate when we graduated from law school.

Our legal education gave us the foundation we needed to become excellent legal practitioners, but few of us have the training necessary to build a successful business. The result is that we work as hard as we can to do excellent legal work, and we wonder why that doesn't result in a growing, thriving legal enterprise. So, we spend more time at the office being the best lawyers we can be, until our family and personal lives suffer and we start to lose our passion for the law.

The truth is, you can create a legal business that is not only growing but is highly profitable, and you can do it while taking time to enjoy life outside the office. The American Academy of Estate Planning Attorneys figured out how to do just that more than two decades ago. Since then, we've helped hundreds of attorneys nation-wide to transform their practices and their lives.

Our secret is simple. Systems.

THE END OF AN ERA

As far back as the medieval guild system, the cost of access to this specialized knowledge was high. No one was privy to it until he underwent a long apprenticeship. Centuries passed and, eventually, law school replaced the apprenticeship. How-ever, the fact remained that only an exclusive few had access to legal knowledge.

Then came the internet.

With it came a massive shift in how people access informa-tion. Thirty years ago, a client who wanted a living trust had little choice but to see an attorney for assistance. Today, that same client can go online and download a fill-in-the-blank form with the click of a button. People no longer need a middle-man to access forms or basic information. The word for this phenomenon is disintermediation, and it means everything has been reduced to a commodity.

ADAPT OR PERISH

How do we compete in this new world? We resist the commo-dity label by differentiating ourselves from other law firms. Too many consumers view every lawyer as just another attor-ney. And who can blame them? Everyone looks the same and uses the same meaningless jargon. We talk about our experience. We offer them our credentials. We promise them the best legal services.

For consumers, one marketing piece blends into another until all lawyers become one grey-suited mass of professionals spouting big words and charging high fees.

If you can't set yourself apart, the only way to compete is by lowering your fees. This sets up a race to the bottom that ends with online service providers charging $99 for a DIY will. And no law firm can compete with those prices.

How can your firm compete in a commodity-focused market? By focusing on one simple truth. Technology is on the march, but it will never eliminate basic human needs. Everyone has the need to:

- Belong
- Be relieved of responsibility for major and complex areas of their lives
- Have a trusted and valued advisor

If you want to survive and thrive in today's market, your firm cannot be just another place to sign documents or get an estate plan. It certainly can't simply be a business structure to pay the rent or put food on your table.

UNDERSTAND YOUR BUSINESS

Instead, it needs to be an invitation to enter a world you've created where you're not just another attorney. This firm should be built on systems designed by you. Every process and activity that takes place within your office walls should bear your signature.

- This is how we answer the phones here
- This is how we generate estate plans
- This is how we greet clients and make them feel welcome
- This is how we conduct meetings

But before you can develop effective systems, you need to know what kind of business you are in. Most attorneys answer this question by saying they're in the business of drafting estate plans, probating estates, administering trusts, or resolving complex disputes. In reality, though you're not in any of these businesses.

You must be in the relationship business.

Take a moment to think about all the legal services a client can acquire without ever having to spend time face-to-face with a professional. Truth be told, we live in a DIY world. Clients can get almost any document online.

The question is, what can't they get online? Content is easy to come by but in so many ways, clients are still flying blind. Sure, a consumer can download an ILIT or a buy-sell agreement, but how do they know they've really covered all the bases—or that there's not another strategy that is more efficient or effective? This is where you come in. Your knowledge, wisdom, and experience allow you to provide muchneeded value, protection, and advice for your clients.

At the Academy, we believe the key to a thriving business is to create a relationship practice instead of one that is merely transactional. One where your business exists to create deep, meaningful, long-term relationships leading to a transformation of your clients' planning expectations. One where you make a sale to get a client, not vice versa.

The legal industry is full of practitioners who have always used a technical, transactional approach. Against this backdrop, our way of doing things is a radical departure. It works because it directly addresses our client's needs and it speaks to them in their language. Clients don't really care about your abilities as a legal technician. They assume that any lawyer should be able to crank out beautiful, flawless documents. So instead of promoting your superior technical skills, you'll be surrounding everything you do for your clients in the bubble of a supportive, indispensible relationship.

With this approach, every part of your firm must tell a consistent story. This is where effective systems, strategies, and tools come in.

The systems will run your practice and keep your vision intact, they will allow you to codify your best practices, and they will allow your practice to rise head and shoulders above the competition.

Believe it or not, most law firms have very few intentional systems. They have no unique way of operating, no overall firm brand.

We have developed 11 Systems to support deep, lasting client relationships — many of them spanning multiple generations. Our Members have used these systems to transform their law firms into practices they love.

 At the Academy, we believe the key to a thriving business is to create a relationship practice instead of one that is merely transactional.

WE CALL IT THE 11 ESSENTIAL SYSTEMS, AND IT CONSISTS OF:

1 *Strategic Planning System:*
Aligning Your Business with Your Personal Values

2 *Finance and Operations Management System:*
Office Set-Up, Employee Handbook, and Managing by the Numbers

3 *A Systems Approach to Leadership:*
Mindset, Unique Abilities, Time Management, Mastery, and more

4 *Staff Accountability and Team Building System:*
Putting the Right People with the Right Skills in the Right Positions

5 *Comprehensive Technology System:*
Integration of Online and Offline Tools to Draft Documents and Manage Your Firm

6 *Integrated Marketing and Public Relations System:*
Multiple Marketing Activities Generating an Endless Supply of Qualified Prospects

7 **Successful Consultations:**
No-Stress Client Engagement System: Predictably Inspiring Consumers to Take Action and Retain Your Firm

8 **Efficient Workflow Systems:**
Drafting, Reviewing and Executing State-of-the-Art Estate Plans

9 **Continuing Legal Education System:**
Staying on the Cutting Edge of Effective Legal Strategies

10 **Ancillary Business System:**
Developing Multiple Sources of Revenue

11 **Staying on the Cutting Edge:**
Participating in a Community of Like-Minded Attorneys: Events, Listserv, Webinars, Calls with Attorneys from Around the Country

It takes these 11 Systems, properly coordinated and executed, to really raise the bar and create the highest quality of life and success in your practice.

The transformation of your law firm starts with the Strategic Planning System, a three-step blueprint that allows you to envision your ideal law firm and lay the groundwork for making that vision a reality.

3 STEPS TO A SUCCESSFUL PLAN

STEP ONE:
**Primary
Aim**

STEP ONE:
**Strategic
Objective**

STEP ONE:
**Organizational
Strategy**

A THREE-STEP SYSTEM FOR TRANSFORMING YOUR LAW FIRM

Every day you wake up and head to the office to practice law. The question is, do you face most days with excitement? Does your career match the vision you had on the day you graduated from law school?

Or, like too many attorneys, did you start out with lofty dreams of a fulfilling career that allows you to make a contribution to your community only to find that, over the years, you've become a slave to the clock—and to the countless "urgent matters" that cross your desk on a daily basis?

> *Alan Kay said, "The best way to predict your future is to invent it." What would your law practice look like if you could create it from scratch?*

You're about to learn a three-step strategy for inventing a law firm that will be uniquely yours. One that combines your personal values and passion with your career and becomes a thriving business that has an indelible influence on everyone around you.

We call this three-step strategy the Strategic Planning System. Unlike long-term planning (which begins with the current status and lays down a path to meet estimated future needs); **strategic planning starts with your desired end and works backward to your current status.**

When you engage in strategic planning, you're systematically envisioning the future you want, and then breaking this vision down into broadly defined goals and a sequence of steps to achieve them. Quite literally, strategic planning lets you dream your desired future and make it your reality.

Ready to get started?

STEP ONE: PRIMARY AIM

The first step in developing a strategic plan for your law firm may seem counterintuitive to you. It involves taking a step back from all the work you've been doing, scheduling some time away from the office, and figuring out what you want your life to look like.

One thing most lawyers have in common is that we're hard workers, and this is usually a virtue. But sometimes it can be our fatal flaw. Particularly when we assume—as many of us do—that if we understand how to do good legal work, we'll automatically know how to run a successful law firm.

This assumption leads to law firm owners who spend countless hours doing what they do best: working in their law firms. They rarely, if ever, take the time to step back for a moment and work on their law firms. Consequently, their firms fail to thrive. And the lawyers themselves spend years muddling through unfulfilling careers.

They find themselves thinking things like:

- "I work too hard"
- "I don't make enough money"
- "I never have enough time"
- "I'm not inspired"

If this sounds familiar to you, it's time to work *on* your business, starting with creating a primary aim. Take some time to really think about the answers to these questions:

- What do you want your life to look like? Not just your workweek, but your life?
- If you could dream it into reality, what would it look like on a day-to-day basis?
- What would your relationship with your family be like? Your friends? Your employees? Your clients? Your community?
- How will people think about you? What words will they use to describe you? How will they feel when they think about you?
- What will you be doing a year from now? In 5 years? 10? 20?
- How much money will you need in order to make this kind of life a reality? When will you need it?

As you pore over the answers to these questions, you'll see the information you need to write your primary aim. It should be a short statement, a couple of sentences that outlines the essence of what your life is about. When you read over your primary aim, it should make you feel energetic, enthusiastic, and committed. Each time you look back at it, you should think, "Yes! This is me!"

This, in turn, will give you a standard to measure your progress as you go about the work of building the law firm—and the life—you have envisioned.

Your primary aim will serve another invaluable purpose. It will give you the confidence to say "no." As you become more successful and your profile in the community rises, your opportunities will increase. If you are not clear about your objectives, you won't be able to discern a good opportunity from a bad one. When your objective is clear, it makes saying no infinitely easier.

Since your primary aim lays the foundation for all your decision making, there is no agonizing over whether each new opportunity is your golden opportunity. Guess what? Your golden opportunity is the one you created yourself when you formulated your primary aim.

 WE'RE HAPPY TO HELP: if you have questions along the way, do not hesitate to email **Questions@aaepa.com** or call us at **(800)846-1555.**

STEP TWO: STRATEGIC OBJECTIVE

After you have established your primary aim, it's time to focus in on how you'll create the revenue and the owner compensation that will enable you to have the great life you've just imagined. This is your strategic objective, and it is a detailed picture of how your business will serve your primary aim. It may mean fine-tuning the firm you've already created, or it may mean a major overhaul.

The first step in establishing your strategic objective is to banish all assumptions and start with a clean slate. Then, ask yourself some questions.

Are you sure you want to practice law? Some attorneys complete this exercise only to figure out that the practice of law is not where their passion lies. If this is the case for you, we see this as a success because we've helped start you on the path to aligning your passion with your career.

> *As you map out your strategic objective, the thing to keep in mind is that, ultimately, what your clients feel about you and your firm will be the most important factor in your success.*

Assuming you do want to practice law, what practice area will you focus on, and in what geographic area? If you don't have passion for your current practice area, do some soul searching and take time to explore other areas of the law before continuing on your current path.

Where will your office be located, and how many employees will you have at first? Project into the future and see how and when your business will grow. How many offices and employees will you have in 1, 5, or 10 years?

What mix of services will you offer your clients? Speaking of clients, who are your ideal clients? Think about their ages, their income and net worth, and their occupations.

What is your firm's competitive advantage—what unique characteristics do you bring to the table that will draw clients to you and set you apart from other firms in your market?

As you map out your strategic objective, the thing to keep in mind is that, ultimately, what your clients feel about you and your firm will be the most important factor in your success. This is why it is so important that you always let your primary aim guide you in your decision making. It is the heart and soul of your business.

STEP THREE: ORGANIZATIONAL STRATEGY

The third and final step in the Strategic Planning System is to determine your organizational strategy. This is where you fine-tune your plan and develop the blueprint that shows what needs to get done, who is going to do it, and, most importantly, how it will be done. The how involves identifying each goal you want to accomplish, outlining the steps necessary to do it, and developing a system for ensuring those steps are taken.

This means even if the employees within your firm change, the system doesn't. Each task will be done one way—your firm's signature way. The result is that your clients enjoy a steady, consistently excellent level of quality every time they interact with your firm, no matter which person they're interacting with.

> *Mapping out your firm's organizational strategy begins with developing an organizational chart.*

Mapping out your firm's organizational strategy begins with developing an organizational chart. This chart is a written representation of every task performed within your business, with each task assigned to an employee. This allows you to think clearly about what needs to be done and who should be accountable for it.

At first, your name may pepper the organizational chart, because you'll be responsible for the lion's share of the work within your business. However, it shouldn't stay this way for long. With the right planning and preparation, you'll hire and train talented and well-prepared team members who will eventually take over many, if not most, of the day-to-day tasks on your organizational chart.

The next step in your organizational strategy is to establish a set of systems that addresses all of the functions your law firm fulfills on a regular basis.

For example, you'll likely need:

- A system for hiring and training employees
- A system for successfully marketing your firm so you continually have prospective clients,
- A system for ensuring qualified prospects retain your firm
- A system for ensuring you provide your clients with-consistently high-level service

And a host of other systems to ensure your business thrives — and you don't drown in an ever-growing to-do list.

The next step in bringing your ideal law firm to life is laying a solid foundation.

Your office set-up should be well planned and coordinated with your strategic plan, your plan should be communicated clearly to current and future employees using a hiring system and a custom employee handbook, and it is imperative that you be able to measure the health of your firm against proven metrics. We call this managing by the numbers. These are all components of the Finance and Operations Management System.

MANAGING BY THE NUMBERS

How do you manage your law firm's finances?

Even now, many attorneys manage their firms' finances with nothing more than a checkbook and the phone number to the bank. This is a dicey way to operate. If you want a firm that serves you a healthy, growing law firm, a solid financial management system is a must.

So, what should your financial management system look like?

FOUNDATION

The first thing your financial system needs is a solid foundation; a set of tools and processes for making sure you know exactly where you are in relation to your financial goals.

TOOLS

1. Accounting Software

Most Academy Members use QuickBooks.

2. Chart of Accounts

It is important to set up your accounting systems in a way that will allow you to see where you are inrelation to your goals. You must review weekly, monthly and annually. Numbers important to be able to review at each point in time, include:

- Gross Revenue
- Net Revenue
- Number of transactions per revenue type

- Revenue per transaction type (Trusts, Wills, Amendments, Trust Admin, etc)
- Gross Marketing Costs
- Marketing cost per client, per event
- Percentage of gross revenue spent on non-equity staff and attorneys
- Percentage of gross revenue spent on owner's compensation
- Any other "benchmarkable" numbers that will keep you apprised of the health of each area of your practice
- Any other "benchmarkable" numbers that will keep you apprised of the health of each area of your practice

This review doesn't take as long as you'd think. The biggest investment of time in this area is spent setting up the systems in the beginning.

 The Academy provides its members with a Chart of Accounts to classify and track all the money their firm receives and pays out.

The Academy's Chart of Accounts serves a dual purpose: it allows Members to accurately track their firm's finances in the categories their marketing impacts, and it gives them the chance to compare their firm's financials with Member firms across the country.

We give our Member firms the opportunity to voluntarily submit their Profit and Loss Statements at the end of each year. At our annual Spring Summit, we hold a closed-door session where each participating firm can compare numbers, see where they rank, and look at benchmarks for different categories of receipts and expenditures. All of this is done anonymously. As part of this session, a panel of volunteers talks about how they achieved their numbers. Imagine comparing your financials to 60-80 law firms with similar staffing and goals! It's an extraordinary meeting.

3. Bookkeeper
You should not be the bookkeeper for your firm. This job should be delegated to a capable, trustworthy employee. If you don't have someone to delegate to, this responsibility is worth outsourcing.

4. Banker
If you do not have a personal banker, you should find one as soon as possible.

5. Line of Credit
Every business should have a line of credit, just in case. The best time to get a line of credit is when you don't need it.

PROCESS
Your firm should have a defined process for handling and tracking:

- Accounts Payable
- Accounts receivable
- Cash

- Payroll
- Deposits

Make sure you have software backup for this information and that you have a backup to the person or people who handle your accounting.

The Academy's recommendation to assign the bookkeeping and accounting responsibilities to a bookkeeper or accountant does not mean you, as the owner, should not be actively involved.

We highly recommend reviewing accounting reports at least weekly and always go over each number, comparing these numbers to your goals and predictions.

Be actively involved in the accounting but delegate the data entry and other aspects of this responsibility. Be sure to close out each month by the 10th of the next month.

PLANNING AND BENCHMARKS

With a solid foundation in place, it's time to execute.

Daily Number

What is your financial goal for this year, and how do you determine, on any given day, whether you're on track to meet your goal?

We recommend that every law firm have a daily number. Here's how it works:

First, determine your gross revenue goal for the year. The Academy has spent years gathering and evaluating financial information from law firms across the country. We have developed financial benchmarks for all the categories of work typically performed by estate planning and elder law firms; for example, the Academy benchmark for owner's compensation is a minimum of 40% of the firm's annual revenue. We make these benchmarks available to our Members to help them set reasonable goals.

Next, sit down with your calendar and figure out how many days you'll work over the next year. Eliminate weekends and holidays, as well as any other days your office will be closed.

Finally, divide your annual revenue goal by the number of working days in the year. The resulting figure is your daily number. It's the amount of money your firm has to bring in every day to meet your annual revenue goal.

EMPLOYEE PLANNING

Your employees are one of your firm's most valuable resources. They're also one of your biggest expenses. It's important to spend time thinking about the costs of having employees, beyond simply paying salaries and benefits.

Mistakes

Employees' mistakes are not only a cost; they're an investment. We all make mistakes. The key is to learn from them and avoid repeating them. Cultivate an environment where your employee's mistakes are treated as learning experiences, and you'll minimize this cost to your firm.

Training

It's tempting to cut corners when it comes to training your employees. After all, it is expensive to thoroughly, properly train someone. Before you decide to skimp on training, consider the cost of failing to train your employees.

Untrained employees are less productive, they tend to make unnecessary mistakes, and their cost to your firm can be astronomical. On the other hand, the return on investment of proper training is huge.

Wasted Time

It's not an obvious expense, but wasted time is a cost to your law firm. It should be treated as a serious matter. If you think about it, employees who take personal calls, surf the internet, and do other personal tasks at work are stealing from your firm. It might sound harsh, but it is true. When an employee is being paid to work, but is not working, they're taking money from your firm. Employees should use their breaks and lunchtime to deal with personal matters.

Some firms require their employees to turn off their cell phones while they're at work. Other firms have installed software to track employee usage of non-work-related websites. Communicate to your employees that you take this kind of wasted time seriously, and then implement the measures you believe are necessary to limit this expense to your firm.

Other Costs
Don't forget about the costs of human resources issues and sick time; these expenses are often left out of the equation when you are calculating the costs of hiring an employee.

GETTING THINGS DONE
Another aspect of successful planning is establishing systems to make sure things get done on a daily basis.

Activity vs. Accomplishment
Avoid the fatal error of believing that just because everyone in your office is busy, tasks are actually being accomplished. There will always be activity in your business; your job is to know whether the work is being completed. Activity happens when work is in progress with no set completion date.

Accomplishment, on the other hand, happens when tasks are properly delegated with measurable goals and a defined completion date. It is essential that you be a good delegator, and that you follow up on deadlines when you've delegated a task. If you're not good at following up, make sure you have a mechanism for reminding you to do so.

Cycles of Productivity

Everyone experiences cycles of productivity—even you. Be aware of your own peaks and valleys of productivity, and take time off when you feel the need for rejuvenation. No one can constantly perform at peak levels. Measure what your employees do, and be aware of their cycles of productivity, too.

Cross Training

The worst number in business is number one. When there is only one person in your office who knows how things are done, it's a recipe for disaster. It's essential that you have an operations manual for each position and that you cross-train your employees so they know how to do each other's jobs. This way, your office can continue to run smoothly when an employee gets sick, takes vacation time, or is away from work for any other reason.

Hire Slow, Fire Fast

If you have cross-trained your employees, you won't have to rush to replace an employee who leaves your firm. Instead, that person's work will continue to get done while you take your time evaluating candidates and hiring the right person for the position. Hire based on work ethic and attitude; skills can be taught on the job.

Take the pulse of any new employee. Give them an assignment on their first day of work: ask them to send you an email every day for the next 20 days. The email should tell you what they accomplished that day, what challenges they experienced, and what they need so they can do their work effectively. Then, sit back and see what happens. Almost every employee forgets to send at least one email. When this happens, give them one reminder and no more.

At the end of those 20 days, you'll have the pulse of your new employee. If you discover an employee is a bad fit for your firm, do not hesitate to terminate that person. Waiting won't make the job any easier, and having a bad fit is costly. Work doesn't get done the way it should, and keeping someone in the wrong position can create a ripple effect.

GOALS AND ACCOUNTABILITY

There are two keys to accomplishing your goals for your law firm. First, you must be crystal clear in defining your goals, along with the steps you need to take to accomplish them. Second, you have to be accountable.

Goal Setting

Can you articulate the goals you want to accomplish over the next 12 months? What about the next 12 weeks, 12 hours, and 12 minutes?

If you can't articulate your goals, how can you accomplish them or expect others to support you in the achievement of your goals?

Your goals should be specific and should also include some of the following areas of focus:

- Revenue per attorney
- Revenue per person on payroll
- Owner compensation
- Cost per case
- Conversion percentage
- Average transaction amount per client
- Lifetime client value
- Daily number
- And more

Members have access to a computer dashboard that keeps their firm's financial goals and marketing plan in front of them on a consistent basis. This helps them track their progress and stay focused on their goals.

Occasionally the Academy offers an instructional webinar for non-Academy Members to review proven benchmarks for all facets of a law firm's finances.

If you're interested in finding out if the upcoming schedule includes this conversation please email us at Questions@aaepa.com.

ACCOUNTABILITY

Successful business people put pressure on themselves when it comes to attaining their goals. They also know that holding yourself accountable is never as effective as finding another person to hold you accountable.

> *You should have last month's numbers in front of you by the tenth of every month.*

We strongly recommend that Members review their financials on a monthly basis. In fact, you should have last month's numbers in front of you by the tenth of every month. This monthly review, along with a policy that you sign every check that leaves your law firm, keeps you in touch with what is going on in your firm.

![leadership highlighted in green among other words: great leader, and communicati, of leadership, the team memb, the, organi]

Once you've laid the groundwork for your firm's basic operations and finances, it is time to step back and take stock of your job as leader of your law firm.

One of your roles as you take the helm of your new (or newly incarnated) firm will be as a thought leader. It will be up to you to visualize where your practice is headed and to galvanize your employees as you take them in a new direction.

To be an effective leader, you'll need to look at time management, communication, and delegation in new ways. A Systems Approach to Leadership will show you how to do this.

How effective are you as the leader of your law firm? Not as your firm's owner or manager, but as the person who develops a vision for the firm and unites your employees in making that vision a reality?

If you spend most of your time putting out fires, or if you're so busy you don't have time to review your firm's financials every month, you are not leading your law firm effectively.

There are three keys to effective law firm leadership: being an effective communicator, mastering the management of your time and teaching your employees to do the same, and knowing what work to delegate and how to delegate it so the work gets done.

COMMUNICATION

Do your employees know your vision for your firm, and can each employee explain how his or her work contributes to the firm's overall mission?

According to a Covey survey of 23,000 employees, only 37% had a clear understanding of what their organization was trying to do. Worse than that, only 20% could articulate the direct relationship between what they do and what the organization was trying to accomplish.

A successful law firm is powered by a team of employees working together toward a common goal. Your job, as leader of your team, is threefold:

1. Start by having a vision for your firm

You need a compelling "why" for your practice of law—and for your life. What are you trying to accomplish as leader of your law firm, and how will your firm make a unique contribution to the community while supporting the lifestyle you want?

2. Communicate your "why" to your employees

After you've developed a vision for your firm, let your employees in on it. If you are excited about the story of your firm and your plans for its future, your employees will be excited, too.

3. Let each team member know how he or she contributes

It's not enough for your employees to be excited about your overall plans for the firm. Each employee needs to know precisely how his or her work within the firm contributes to its success. Your employees especially need to know and understand your financial goals for the firm, particularly your daily number—the amount of revenue the firm needs to bring in each day to meet your annual gross revenue goal.

TIME MANAGEMENT

With a solid foundation in place, it's time to execute.

Time is one of your most valuable assets, and you should protect it. It is all too easy to lose track of time and let it slip away. Successful businesspeople are excellent managers of their time. This is not a common trait. In fact, most people have no idea how they spend their time.

Before you can come up with a plan to manage your time, you need to understand how and where you're spending it. In other words, you need to audit your time. A great way to do this is to keep a time log for two weeks. Here's how:

- For a period of two weeks, write down everything you do each day, along with the amount of time you spend doing it. Include sleeping, eating, getting ready in the morning, and every other activity.

- After two weeks, categorize each activity. For your time at work, you can create categories like Administration and Management, First Consultations, Marketing, Downtime, or any other categories that work for you. The idea is to get a clear picture of how you spend the majority of your time, and whether you're spending it productively.

- For each at-work category, ask yourself whether it qualifies as working in your business (drafting documents, meeting with prospects, deepening your relationship with existing clients) or working on your business (planning, analyzing numbers, enhancing your education).

Many attorneys find they're doing work they should delegate, freeing them up to work on growing their business. Others find they are losing too much of their time to distractions.

EMAIL

Email can be an excellent tool, but it's easy to let it run your life, particularly when the first thing you do each morning is check your inbox. One way to minimize distractions is to stop looking at your email in the morning. There are a number of good reasons for this:

1. Ignorance is bliss

If you don't know about other peoples emergencies, you're not unnecessarily worried and distracted as you go about your business.

2. Email is not YOUR to do list

Your inbox contains other peoples' requests for your time. You need to be in charge of your schedule, and remain focused on your goals.

3. Email is an excuse for not having direction

When you're distracted by email, it is easy to sacrifice your time to what might be urgent, and forget to do the things that are truly important.

4. When you answer email quickly, you train everyone around you to expect a quick response every time.

5. Email absorbs more time than you think

Consider how many emails you send and receive each day; let's say it's 100. If you spend two minutes on each message, you're sacrificing 200 minutes of your day—nearly 3 1/2 hours—to email.

If email is a problem for you, try this: Each evening, before you leave the office, write down the top three most important things you need to accomplish the next day. When you get to the office the next morning, don't check your email until you've accomplished your top three.

MULTITASKING

You might not be as great a multitasker as you think. Studies have shown that multitasking creates a 40% reduction in productivity, a 10-point drop in IQ, and it creates stress.

Instead of multitasking, focus on one task at a time. It's nice to do one thing, without distraction, and do it well. It's also nice when your employees and clients have your full attention, rather than having to compete with your phone or your email.

> *Instead of multitasking, focus on one task at a time.*

The next time you have a conversation with someone, try putting down your cell phone and turning off your computer screen. You'll both benefit from the lack of distractions.

DELEGATION

Are you a control freak when it comes to your law firm? Too many attorneys fail to put their time to its highest and best use. Instead, they spend their time doing work their employees should do.

There are two—and only two—types of work you should do.

1. You should do the work that can only be done by an attorney.
2. You should do only those things you do best.

Every other task should be delegated to your employees, based on their individual strengths. If you don't know what your strengths are, it's easy to find out. Go to **www.kolbe.com** and take the Kolbe A™ Index. Then, have everyone in your office take it, too. The Kolbe A™ Index is an online test that measures your instinctive way of doing things, and identifies the ways you'll be most productive.

Finding out what your strengths are allows you to complement yourself in areas where you're not as strong. Ideally, you'll be able to delegate tasks that fall into your weak areas to a team member who has a natural aptitude for them.

HAPPY EMPLOYEES

Are your employees happy, energetic members of your law firm team, or do they find their jobs miserable and unfulfilling?

According to business consultant Patrick Lencioni, there are three signs of a miserable job, each with its own solution:

- **Anonymity.** If your employees don't think you know them and what's going on in their lives, or if they think you don't care about them, their work will be unfulfilling. They won't be motivated when they come to the office in the morning. The solution to the problem of anonymity is simple. Take the time to get to know your employees and learn about their lives. Let them know you appreciate them, and they will not feel anonymous.

- **Irrelevance.** Employees believe their jobs are irrelevant when they do not know that their work matters and they don't see how other people's lives are impacted by how well they do their job. The way to ensure your employees don't feel that their jobs are irrelevant is to make sure everyone in your firm knows how their work has a direct impact on your clients.

- **Immeasurement.** Immeasurement happens when there is a lack of clear goals for your employees to accomplish and when they have no clear way to measure their performance. When the only measure of their success is your mood, employees feel powerless to control or influence their careers.

It's not difficult to solve this problem. Set clear, defined goals for your employees and give them feedback on the work they do.

AUDIT YOUR LAW FIRM

You might read this report and immediately identify what is missing in your law firm. On the other hand, you might know that things are not running smoothly at the office, or that your firm is not performing as well as it could, but you can't put your finger on the reason. Sometimes the problem is a disconnect between what you think is being done in your law firm and what is actually being done.

When all you're doing is putting out fires, when you don't have time to properly manage your staff, you're rushing through client consultations, and you're not keeping up with your firm's financials or your marketing calendar... these are signs that you are off target.

With your approach to leadership in place, it is time to consider how you will go about hiring and training employees.

In many law firms, hiring and training are haphazard at best. When a need presents itself, the firm runs an ad, conducts a few interviews, and chooses a new employee. This new employee is usually selected based on skill and experience. The new hire comes to work, receives a few days' worth of training from the person leaving the position, and is left to sink or swim. Too often, there is more sinking than swimming.

Academy attorneys do things a little differently. They use our Staff Accountability and Team Building System to hire, train, and monitor employee performance. Hiring is conducted with an eye toward personality, rather than a focus on skill or experience. Each employee knows what to do, how to do it, and why they're doing it. More than that, employees are teammates, actively invested in the growth of the law firm. With this system, each role in your firm is filled by the right person and work consistently gets done the right way—your signature way—regardless of the circumstances.

HOW TO PUT THE RIGHT PEOPLE WITH THE RIGHT SKILLS IN THE RIGHT POSITIONS

Do you have an employee who is the backbone of your firm, someone who does such a great job and knows the inner workings of your office so well that you'd be lost without that person?

Many attorneys brag about that one employee without whom they'd be lost. In reality, this isn't a virtue. What happens when this "star employee" gets sick or finds another position? They're gone, and your firm is in trouble!

How do you avoid this problem? You transition your firm from one that's people-dependent to one that's system-dependent, and you make sure you have fabulous people running your systems.

Having a system-dependent firm does not mean your employees are any less capable, less important, or less worthy of acclaim and appreciation. In fact, the opposite is true. When the foundation of your firm's operations is an integrated set of effective systems, your employees are freed up to perform at the highest possible level. They don't have to worry about figuring out how to greet clients, assemble documents, do the final signing, or any other basic function within your firm, because there are systems in place for these things. Your firm is your invention, so you get to develop your own unique, systematic way of accomplishing your work.

Here's how you transition from an employee-based firm to a systems-based firm:

DEVELOP A FIRM ORGANIZATIONAL CHART

Your firm's organizational chart is a written representation of every task that must be accomplished within your office.

At the top of your chart is a box with your name in it. You are the firm's partner, president, or CEO, and every task performed within your firm is performed under your leadership. Below this box is a series of boxes, one for each department within your firm. Below each department's box are more boxes. These represent the tasks the department performs on a regular basis. You'll populate these boxes with the names of the employees who are responsible for each task.

VISION: ORGANIZATIONAL CHART

Consider staffing based on the Academy's benchmarks for Revenue per Employee and Revenue per Attorney.

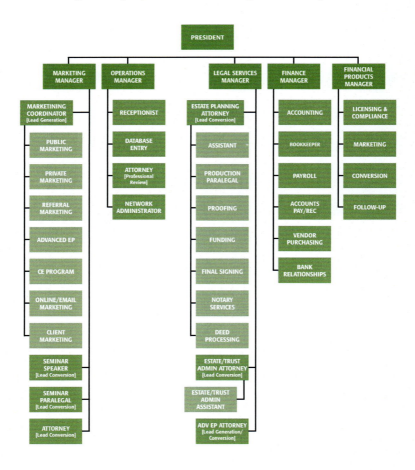

At first, your name may be in most of the boxes. That's okay. As your firm grows and matures, you'll be able to delegate the majority of tasks to trustworthy, well-trained employees.

HAVE A SYSTEM FOR HIRING NEW EMPLOYEES

Chances are you've always used the same method most law firms use for hiring new employees. You run an ad and wait for the resumes to pour in. Next, you review all the resumes and narrow them down to a list of possible prospects. Then, you schedule one-on-one interviews with each possible prospect in order to find the one candidate who is the right fit for the position.

In many cases, you know within the first ten seconds of an interview whether the person sitting in front of you is a real candidate. What happens if it's immediately and glaringly obvious that there's no way you want to hire the person you're interviewing? You can't end the meeting after ten seconds, so you sit there politely until the interviewee feels like you're seriously considering them.

This approach is a waste of time. The Academy suggests an alternative; one that has produced stellar results for our Members:

THE GROUP INTERVIEW

The group interview offers a number of advantages over individual interviews with each potential candidate for a position within your firm:

- It weeds out unfit candidates
- It allows you to promote your firm's culture and history
- It lets you see who shines in a group, so you can select thosestars for a one-on-one interview

Conducting a successful group interview isn't hard. After all the candidates are seated in your conference room, you come in, introduce yourself, and tell the cultural story of your firm and engage the candidates in what it means to possibly work for your firm. Then, you ask open-ended questions about what interested the candidates in this position.

You should have your key team members watching the interview so they can determine whether they want each candidate as part of your firm's team. After the group interview ends, you'll work with your team members to narrow the candidates down to a few obvious choices and have individual interviews with just those people.

HAVE A SYSTEM FOR WEEKLY STAFF MEETINGS

With your team in place, your attention should turn to team building. One way to accomplish this is to have weekly team meetings. Here are a few keys to successful staff meetings:

First, you should not lead the meetings.
The purpose of these meetings is to encourage communication and interactivity among your employees. Meetings should never be a lecture from the boss. Instead, assign responsibility for the meeting to an employee, and have this responsibility rotate among your employees. Of course, your employee should clear the meeting's agenda with you in advance, but you should attend the meeting solely as a participant.

Second, meetings should be a break from the drudgery of the 9 to 5 workday.

Employees should share what's going on, tell each other their success stories and new ideas, and cultivate a sense of family.

Third, staff meetings don't always have to follow the same pattern.
Try ordering a pizza lunch or set aside some time to discuss a book. Make meetings something your staff looks forward to.

> *Weekly team meetings should be a break from the drudgery of the 9 to 5 workday.*

Aside from weekly team meetings, there are countless ways to cultivate an environment of community, positivity, and gratitude. For example:

- Have periodic fun activities. Go bowling, see a movie together, or go to happy hour.
- Set aside time to have periodic dinners with each employee.
- Have an annual retreat to acknowledge the contributions each of your team members have made to the firm, to each other, and to the community.

BUILD YOUR TEAM IN OTHER WAYS

In addition to weekly team meetings and periodic out-of-office activities, there are a number of things you can do to build a strong, positive, productive team.

HAVE A SYSTEM FOR MEASURING YOUR EMPLOYEES' EFFECTIVENESS

Each of your employees should know exactly what is expected of them and exactly how they contribute to your firm's overall success. With clear expectations and regular reviews, you can keep your finger on the pulse of what's really happening in your firm, and your employees won't have to guess at what they do well and what areas need improvement.

HAVE A CROSS-TRAINING SYSTEM

You should have an operations manual—a detailed list—of what everyone in your firm does. This way, if an employee leaves, you can hire the right person to fit into the position and they'll know exactly what to do and how to do it.

By the same token, you should make sure your employees know each other's jobs. With a cross-training system, there is always someone in your office who can fill in if an employee is sick, leaves your firm, or is absent for another reason. With the right hiring and team building systems, you'll have an office that runs like a well-oiled machine. Even better, you and your staff will be able to have fun while you're serving the community and your clients.

Does your firm currently have the technology to provide the seamless service and error-free documents today's clients demand? What about practice management and financial tracking?

INTEGRATION OF ONLINE AND OFFLINE TOOLS TO DRAFT DOCUMENTS AND MANAGE YOUR LAW PRACTICE

Your law firm's technology system is the glue that holds much of your business together. You use technology to keep records; to communicate with colleagues, clients, and employees; and to draft documents.

If you do not have a state-of-the-art technology system—one that integrates tools to draft documents and manage your firm—you're wasting time and money.

Out-of-date technology, or lack of an integrated system, can mean all kinds of headaches for you as a law firm owner. Without a system, it is too easy for contact information and other important client details to get lost, for commitments to fall between the cracks, and for deadlines to be missed.

These tools fall into four principal areas:

1. Relational Database*

We built CounselPro™, the Academy's software, solely for estate planning firms. Look for software that is designed specifically for what you do. You need to track and retrieve data, reports and marketing activities, along with document and workflow status with all of this in mind:

- Prospects
- Clients
- Vendors
- Events and Results

- Correspondence
- Marketing Expenses
- Documents
- Firm-Wide Benchmarks
- To Do's and Notes

When you first make contact with a prospect, a client, or a vendor, that person's information is entered into your software. From that point forward, all of your interactions are recorded, organized, and stored so you can access the information you need when you need it. This level of organization helps you nurture and maintain lifelong relationships with your clients and others in your community.

The same is true for your firm's financials, as well as your marketing activities. Everything goes into CounselPro™, where there are tools for storing and analyzing it to help you maximize your firm's efficiency and profitability.

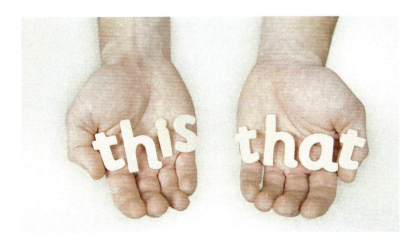

2. Comprehensive Document Assembly Program*

It is equally important to have software linked to your database that produces all the legal documents your clients will be needing. These documents, for most estate planning and elder law attorneys include:

- Revocable Living Trusts
- Amendments
- Restatements
- ILIT's
- Wills
- Special Needs Trusts
- Medicaid Trusts
- Trust Administration letters and documents
- Funding Letters and other documentation

Consider how your documents will be kept up to date. This is a major concern for many attorneys. It takes access to a team to make sure all changes in the law are reflected in your documents. Our belief is that the Attorney should be the CEO and the Counsellor in the law firm, not the researcher or document production paralegal or marketing coordinator.

*The Academy has built a database and document assembly program that link together, removing the need for double entry. This software is called CounselPro™ and is available to Members only.

Email <u>Questions@aaepa.com</u> and ask us to send you a demo of this software.

3. Interactive, Content Rich Website

You need a strong online presence, and the foundation of that is an interactive, content rich website that ranks high on search engines like Google. It is no longer enough to have a website that looks like an online brochure. Your law firm website needs to be complete with onsite search engine optimization. Websites need to be easy to navigate, offer lots of free tips to consumers, have an attractive layout and theme, along with lots of original articles and blog posts with appropriate tags and keywords.

When consumers ask for reports or newsletters, or perhaps subscribe to your blog, you need to have the ability to have auto-responder emails sent automatically to your staff as well as to the consumer. It alerts staff early so appropriate follow up can take place and the consumer's email will make them feel like they're engaged with an attention to detail type law firm.

> *A word of caution: SEO and Website Building "Guru's" are a dime a dozen. Everyone's an expert. Be sure to get complete quotes up front and check references. Check more than one!*

4. AUTOMATED TOOLS TO STAY IN TOUCH

After a client, a vendor, or another professional (we call them Centers of Influence) begins a relationship with your firm, it's essential that you stay in touch.

Mail Merge*

CounselPro™ has a mail merge feature with form letters to notify clients and prospects of meetings and appointments, changes in the law, special seminars, and more. After an individual's information is entered into the system, all you should have to do is choose the appropriate letter from your software. The letter will print out ready for signature with all the appropriate fields filled in.

eAlerts*

eAlerts should be designed to help you nurture your centers of influence and provide consistent communication with clients and others in your database. The Academy provides eAlerts that feature topical information designed for referring professionals, as well as eAlerts that include consumer-friendly topics for clients and prospects. These alerts are typically written by our Legal Education team. There are subscription based electronic newsletters that can provide you copy as well. Again, attorneys need to reserve their time for running the practice and counselling clients... not writing marketing material, even if the material requires a little legal knowledge. Be clear about how you spend your time.

Greeting Cards*

We cannot emphasize enough, the importance of creating a "wow" experience for your clients. When you have a client feel something warm when your name or the law firm name comes up, you've won a client for life.

These "wow" experiences are not typically over the top efforts as much as they are a constant trickle of attention. The Academy has collaborated with Send Out Cards so our Members can easily send economical, professionally designed greeting cards to clients, prospects, and others at a discount. We encourage our Members to use these cards for a variety of occasions, including:

- Birthdays, anniversaries and holidays
- Seminar announcements
- Client review notices
- Client signing photos

Autoresponders*

Autoresponders are a hassle-free way to make contact with people who visit your website. The Academy has pre-written autoresponders available to Members. When a client visits a Member's website and clicks on the "Trust Administration" tab, they'll be taken to a landing page where they can see a short video and read a little about trust administration. They also have the option to enter their contact information and receive a free report. At this point, a series of autoresponders is sent to the visitor. The first email thanks the visitor for their interest, and then six more emails, spaced several days apart, are sent. The emails can address any topic from inviting a visitor to come to a seminar to asking them to come in for a consultation. All of these emails are pre-written and auto-mated, so Members don't have to do any extra work.

The Academy's integrated, state-of-the-art technology system makes it easy to gather client information, draft documents, track and analyze your firm's finances and marketing plan, and stay in touch with prospects, clients, and others. This lets you manage your law firm and nurture lasting relationships with your clients and the people in your community efficiently and without unnecessary stress.

 The Academy has tested and designed all aspects of our Members' websites, SEO Services, autoresponder usage as well as online newsletters and client touches. Access to these tools are just a small part of Membership but a huge part of a law firm's success.

With the nuts and bolts in place, you are geared up to welcome throngs of new clients. Where will you find these new clients? They're all around you. you'll reach out to them and win them over with our integrated Marketing and Public Relations System.

TAKING THE MYSTIQUE OUT OF MARKETING

Marketing. Either you love it, or you hate it. Whatever your feelings about selling your firm's services, the fact is that revenue is the lifeblood of your business. The best way to ensure that you have a steady, predictable revenue stream is to have an integrated marketing system—one that uses a number of strategies and methods to attract the right clients to your firm.

Here's how it should work:

STEP ONE: IDENTIFY YOUR TARGET MARKETS

Before you can develop a marketing strategy, you need to know to whom you are marketing. It does no good to create a fabulous marketing campaign if you aren't clear about who your ideal client is.

We believe the best way to do this is to create a detailed picture—an avatar—of your ideal client. Begin by getting your entire team involved. Call a team meeting and let your employees know that the purpose of the meeting will be to create a profile of your firm's perfect client. Ask your staffers to come to the meeting prepared with everything they know about the people they see day in and day out. At the meeting, compare notes on:

- Your ideal client's income range
- Where they work
- Where they live
- Their hobbies
- Their political views

- Where they shop: is it Walmart? Target? Neiman Marcus?
- What magazines they read
- Where they take vacations: Do they fly to New York for the weekend, drive to the Grand Canyon during the summertime, or take an annual shopping trip to Europe?
- Are they single or married?
- How old are they?

Identifying your ideal client is an essential foundational activity. Everyone in your firm needs to be absolutely clear on what your target market is and what your ideal client looks like. If you offer multiple services, you'll likely have multiple target markets.

STEP TWO: CALCULATE THE LIFETIME VALUE OF YOUR CLIENTS

What is each of your clients worth to your law firm? When you sit down to decide how much money you are willing to devote to bringing in a new client, do not focus solely on the value of that client's first transaction with your firm.

Look beyond the first transaction and consider how much money the client will spend with your firm from the moment you meet them until you no longer have a relationship. A client is not simply a transaction in the form of a Will or a Trust. Consider the Restatements, Amendments, Elder Law Services, and Post Mortem Services the typical client may need throughout their lifetime. Calculating the potential revenue from all of these services gives you the lifetime value of your client. And if you develop a multigenerational relationship with a client's family, that value spans more than a lifetime.

When you think about your clients in terms of their lifetime value to your firm, two things happen:

- First, you begin to structure your marketing budget with an eye toward the full value your client's represent to your firm, rather than focusing on the value of a single transaction.

- Second, realizing your clients' true worth tends to change how you feel toward them and how you treat them. This, in turn, has a huge impact on your clients' experience with your firm.

STEP THREE: CREATE A UNIQUE PLANNING PROCESS

Do your clients come to you simply to get a set of documents? If so, your firm might be in trouble. Think about your competition—the law firm down the street, online services like Legal Zoom—they all offer "legal documents." There are more than one million lawyers nationwide, and in most clients' eyes, we're all about the same.

When clients can't differentiate based on quality, they tend to make comparisons based on price. Competing on price is a losing proposition for you, and it prevents your clients from recognizing the true value of your firm.

YOU HAVE TO BE UNIQUE

One way to do this is to let clients know that your law firm creates a unique plan for each of its clients, and does so while offering unparalleled service every step of the way. This way, clients and prospective clients can identify the special value they're getting from your firm.

One method for accomplishing this is to bundle your services and package them into a unique system. For example, some Academy Member firms offer a Six-Step Family Legacy Wealth Planning System. Here's what's included:

1. A Consultation and Roadmap
2. Plan Design
3. Plan Development
4. Plan Execution and Delivery
5. Plan Asset Transfer and Funding
6. Lifetime Communication and Updates

It is hard to compare a bare bones set of documents with a six-step planning system. If you meet with your staff and develop your own system, you'll be able to demonstrate to your clients how your firm stands head and shoulders above the competition.

In fact, when a prospective client calls and asks your fee for a Living Trust, your answer can be, "The documents are free; that's not what we charge for. We charge for the peace of mind of going through a six-step Legacy Wealth Planning process. Would you like to come in for a consultation?"

This sets you up to become a client's family attorney, instead of just the lawyer who did their Trust.

YOUR FIRM'S MARKETING PLAN

After you've gone through the preliminary steps to identify your target market, fully understand the lifetime value of your clients, and lay the foundation for setting your firm apart from the competition, it's time to establish a marketing plan.

It's easy to be intimidated by the idea of marketing, until you realize marketing is simply the process whereby people get to know, like, and trust you. More than that, marketing is a science. It is the science of getting people to:

1. **Sample Your Services:** A great way to do this is via a Trust Planning Seminar. This lets prospective clients experience firsthand how experienced you are, how well spoken and organized you are, and how well you respond to clients' questions and concerns.

2. **Buy Your Services:** This happens when a client meets with you for an initial consultation and decides to retain your law firm.

3. **Continue Buying Your Services:** This happens after you've designed a client's initial estate plan, and they take advantage of the amendments, restatements, and other services your firm offers.

The Academy helps its Members master the science of marketing by offering a variety of systems and services. This lets Members quickly identify prospective clients who are interested in the firm's message, provide services tailored to their clients' needs, and diligently track the results of the firm's marketing efforts—making it easy to weed through approaches that don't work and repeat successful approaches with consistently predictable results.

The first step toward having an endless stream of qualified prospective clients is to establish an integrated marketing plan. Too many law firms are one-trick ponies. They focus on one marketing strategy rather than diversifying their efforts to reach clients. Inevitably, that marketing strategy—whether it's estate planning seminars, running newspaper ads, or some other approach—hits a speed bump, and the number of prospective clients reached by the firm dwindles.

The cure for this is to spread your marketing around to create multiple marketing streams. Successful marketing is a numbers game. If you have the right information, you can calculate mathematically what it will take for you to reach your revenue goals.

Here's How Academy Attorneys Do It

STEP ONE: ANALYZE LAST YEAR'S MARKETING INFORMATION

If you have been tracking the results of your marketing efforts, you'll gather last year's tracking information, along with last year's financial reports and a list of all the marketing tools and options available to you.

With this information in front of you, you can take your past tracking results and calculate the total revenue from each of your marketing campaigns. This allows you to identify which marketing efforts you want to repeat, note what needs to be revised, and remove campaigns that didn't work. After you begin tracking your marketing efforts, you'll be able to identify the percentage of success each marketing campaign represents.

For example, you should know what percentage of people make appointments after you present an estate planning seminar. Let's assume 33% of seminar attendees make appointments, and of those, at least 80% keep their appointments. Let's further assume that 80% of those who keep their appointments decide to retain your firm.

Armed with this information, you can ask this threshold question. To retain X clients per month, how many people do you need to be in front of?

All you need to do is figure out the math: If 20 people attend your seminar, and 33% make appointments, the seminar will generate 7 appointments. If 80% of these appointments are kept, you'll meet with 6 prospective clients. And if 80% of clients retain the firm, you'll have 5 new clients as a result of your seminar.

This strategy makes it easy to visualize what you need to do.

STEP TWO: CREATE A MARKETING CALENDAR

The Academy recommends that you maintain a marketing calendar, planning your marketing activities one year in advance. We even provide a marketing calendar template to our Members. Here's how it works:

You lay out all 12 months on your conference table, and begin by marking off holidays, major sporting events, and other days that are not conducive to marketing activities.

Then, you start inserting routine marketing tasks, such as:

- Sending out eAlerts
- Sending newsletters, by mail as well as digitally
- Activities that worked last year
- Continuing education courses
- Public and private speaking engagements

Make sure to allow enough time between marketing activities to schedule consultations with your clients, and then take another look at your marketing calendar and calculate your marketing fees.

Next, calculate the potential revenue from the activities you've scheduled, and make any necessary adjustments and compare

your planned efforts to your goals. Simple as that, you have a year-long marketing strategy planned and ready to implement.

ACADEMY TOOLS AND SYSTEMS

The Academy offers a wide variety of tools and systems to help its Members plan and implement successful marketing strategies. Our systems focus on four areas:

1. Generating Client Referrals

Before clients will refer you to their friends, family Members, and colleagues, you have to prove that you're referable. The Academy offers a Seven-Step Client Referral System that shows Members how to establish themselves as trusted, referable professionals. The system also provides easy-to-execute steps for successfully asking clients for referrals.

2. Obtaining Referrals from Other Professionals (Your Centers of Influence)

With Academy support, Members learn how to establish themselves as experts as they interact with financial advisors and other professionals. They also have the opportunity to take advantage of our five principal marketing tools for reaching out to these centers of influence. The tools include:

- eAlerts
- Special reports
- CE courses
- Monthly newsletter
- Client in Common letter

3. Presenting Informative Public Seminars

We provide our Members with all the tools they need to present up-to-date, informative seminars to private or public groups. A few of our seminar topics include:

- Legacy Wealth Planning
- Basic Estate Planning
- Irrevocable Life Insurance Trust
- Funeral Trust Seminar
- Estate Planning for Small Business Owners
- Pet Planning
- Lawsuit and Asset Protection
- Medicaid Planning Workshop

4. Optimizing Your Online Presence

The internet has changed the way clients find attorneys. Today, the vast majority of Internet users go online to find a lawyer, and 65% of people begin their search for an attorney online. Without a visible online presence, you're missing out on a large and growing portion of the market.

That's why we offer our Members a range of online marketing services, from establishing effective law firm websites to increasing their online profile with search engine optimization. No matter how you feel about marketing, the Academy offers all the support, systems, and tools you need to increase your firm's visibility and attract a steady stream of well-qualified prospects.

The Academy offers a wide variety of tools and systems to help its Members plan and implement successful marketing strategies.

For a closer look at the vast amount of tools available, email Questions@aaepa.com and ask us to send you additional information on marketing.

As this steady stream of prospects makes its way through your doors, you'll need a way to consistently and predictably turn those prospects into clients. if you've practiced law for any length of time, you know that's easier said than done.

It is incredibly frustrating to invest time, money, and energy into having a prospective client book an initial appointment, only to be told "no thanks," or, worse yet, to have the appointment cancelled at the last minute.

Our No-Stress Client Engagement System minimizes this frustration by truly systematizing the initial consultation process. The system emphasizes your firm's unique value, it helps you weed out prospects you don't want to work with, and it prioritizes relationship building and counseling skills.

WIN THEM OVER: THE SECRET TO SUCCESSFUL FIRST CONSULTATIONS

The initial consultation. It's a critical step in your relationship with a prospective client.

> *Our No-Stress Client Engagement System minimizes frustration by truly systematizing the initial consultation process.*

You've already made quite an investment in this budding relationship. You've spent time and money on a marketing campaign. Maybe you've hosted an estate planning seminar. Whatever you've done so far, it has been fruitful. You have a face-to-face meeting scheduled with your prospective client. The hour or two you spend in this meeting will determine whether the relationship progresses.

With so much invested already, why would you wing it? Yet this is how many lawyers approach initial consultations, often with less-than optimal results. The outcome of this approach is inconsistent results, high stress levels for you and your prospective clients, and retention rates that just aren't as high as they could be.

The alternative is to have a system for how each attorney in your firm conducts initial consultations. With an effective system, you and your clients benefit. Here's how:

- **Consistency.** The right system makes you consistent, and when you're consistent, you can expect predictable results. Your stress levels go down, and your retention rates go up. This increases your bottom line and it enables you to help more families with their estate planning needs.

- **Counselling.** The right system helps you uncover your prospects' true needs, showcase your skills as a counselor, and identify which prospects are a good fit for your firm.

- **Client Expectations.** The right system helps you set and manage client expectations from the very beginning. It also helps you follow through on the promises you make, unfailingly keeping your word. This helps you reduce everyone's stress levels, and it turns your law firm into a positive, comfortable environment for you, your staff, and your clients.

THE FOUNDATIONS OF A SUCCESSFUL CONSULTATION SYSTEM

Before you can implement any system effectively, you need to lay the foundation for a good relationship with your clients. This starts before a new guest ever sets foot in your office, when you begin creating an environment of trust and rapport.

TRUST

It's not that complicated to create an environment of trust within your law firm. The key is consistency; doing what you say you'll do. Setting reasonable expectations, and then meeting or exceeding them. Peoples' expectations—particularly their expectations of lawyers—have fallen so low that you can thrill your clients just by keeping your word.

In addition to doing what you say, you need to consider the way you present yourself to clients and prospective clients. Are you just another run-of-the-mill lawyer, or are you an authority in your area of practice? If you are a confident, self-assured authority—and you have the credentials to prove it—you're that much further ahead when it comes to winning your prospects' trust. If you can't confidently call yourself an authority, do something about it! Become an authority by speaking or writing on your area of law. Not just once or twice, but routinely.

The Academy offers its Members a variety of tools to help them consistently meet or exceed their clients' expectations and to establish themselves as authorities through speaking engagements and publication opportunities.

RAPPORT

From the moment a client encounters your firm, you're either building rapport or you're not. The real question is whether people feel okay or not okay as they interact with you and your team members. Your job is to make prospects feel okay, and you can accomplish this in a number of ways:

- **A Warm Environment.** When a prospective client walks into your office, they should be warmly greeted by name. Your waiting area should feel welcoming and comfortable, with current reading materials and refreshments ready and available.

- **A Prompt, Focused Attorney.** It is imperative to be on time for client consultations and to be clear-minded and focused throughout your meeting. You should have a standard way of preparing for every client consultation so you're alert and on your game. This communicates respect for your prospective clients and it lets them know they can trust you.

- **A Comfortable Attorney.** When you meet a new prospective client, are you confident and relaxed, or are you stiff and nervous? If you're nervous, your guest will be, too. Think of an initial consultation as a dinner party. You're the host, and your job is to make your guests as comfortable as possible.

A WORD ABOUT ATTITUDE

Do you approach initial consultations like a desperate salesperson, or like a highly skilled professional who is there to help a family seeking advice? Your attitude can mean the difference between success and failure. If you come across like a salesperson, you will alienate prospective clients.

Here's the secret to not acting as if you're desperate: approach each initial consultation like you're independently wealthy and you don't need the business. Go into the meeting to find out how you can help the person you're meeting with, as well as whether they're a good fit for your firm. Now that these preliminaries are in place, it's time to talk about the Academy's No-Stress Client Engagement System.

THE FIVE-STEP SYSTEM

It's the day of the consultation. Your receptionist has warmly greeted your prospective clients by name, and they're seated comfortably in your lobby, awaiting the prompt start of your meeting. When it's time for the meeting to start, you'll come to the lobby to greet your guests and escort them to your conference room, or you'll have your receptionist escort them to the conference room.

Step One: The Upfront Agreement

The upfront agreement is the starting point for your consultation. You'll take a few moments to review some essentials with your prospects, and to ensure everyone is on the same page from the beginning.

You'll confirm the time allotted for the meeting, and make sure that still works for your prospects. Then, you'll briefly go over the agenda for the consultation: you'll have questions to ask about your prospects and their needs, they'll likely have questions for you, and then you'll determine what type of estate plan meets their needs. At this point, your prospects will make a decision. They'll either want to get started, or they won't, and saying "no" is okay.

Emphasizing the need to make a decision, and the fact that it's okay to say "no," is important for setting the tone of the meeting. You want to make sure every prospect makes a decision, and making it clear it's okay if that decision is "no" removes the pressure and makes your prospects feel comfortable. Finally, you'll end your upfront agreement by asking your prospective client whether there's anything they'd like to add to the agenda.

Step Two: Qualification

The second step of the system is all about finding out why your prospect is sitting in front of you. We call this step the Truth Funnel, and here's how you do it:

1. **Listen very carefully** for any issue, concern, or pain your prospect may have; then
2. **Uncover** the financial or economic impact of allowing that issue to go unaddressed; finally
3. **Get to the emotional center** of the issue. People make decisions with their emotions, and then they justify their decisions with the facts.

There are two keys to mastering the Truth Funnel.

First, you need to ask open-ended questions. For example, instead of asking, "What are your children's names" or, "Do you own any real estate?" you should ask questions like:

- What prompted you to come in today?
- What needs do you have that we can help you with?
- What inspired you to make an estate plan?

Second, you need to listen more than you talk. The first consultation is about getting your client to open up and talk. Your job is to listen very carefully for a problem you can help them resolve. Once you identify a problem, go through the steps of the pain-gain funnel. Then, listen some more and identify another issue. Repeat this process until you and your prospect have identified and discussed all the issues that need to be addressed.

Step Three: Investment

Contrary to the television ads for do-it-yourself Wills and Trusts, an effective, professionally crafted estate plan requires a substantial investment of both time and money on the part of our clients. We know it, but it's something they might not realize at first.

That's why we need to spend some time during the initial consultation to set reasonable expectations. You do this by saying, "Assuming you were sure we could exceed your expectations in all your main areas of concern and we're looking at an investment of $X, would you choose to go forward with your planning? In addition to the financial investment, we're also going to need 5 to 8 hours of your time to work with us in accomplishing your goals. Are you comfortable with that?"

Simple as that. The costs are out there, and your prospect has a framework for what kind of investment to expect.

Step Four: Decision

Often, our Members find they can omit this step. At this point in the consultation, you need to make sure there's no one else who needs to be consulted before your prospect can make a decision. Occasionally, a prospect will be hesitant to start an estate plan because they want input from a third party. Maybe it's their daughter who is a CPA or their friend the real estate attorney.

If you're faced with this roadblock, there are two choices. Often, the real issue isn't the need for your prospect to consult with anyone else; instead, they're uncomfortable with some aspect of the meeting thus far. If this is the case, you may be able to go back, ask some additional questions, and address this discomfort.

Otherwise, get your prospect to tell you who they need to talk to, what they need to ask these people about, and how long they need to accomplish this. Then, write this information down so everyone has an action plan and no one is left hanging. If your prospect leaves your office without a clearly defined plan of action, the chances that you'll ever see them again plummet.

Step Five: The Clear Next Step

This is the part of your consultation where you let your prospect know your firm's process for getting them from the present moment to the signing of the final documents. After you outline the exact steps your prospect can expect, he or she will likely be ready to proceed.

NEXT STEPS

Now that you're familiar with the system, what do you do with it?

The Academy's No Stress Client Engagement System is a huge departure from many attorneys' default way of doing things. Our Members have found that it takes practice to fully implement the system in their law firms.

That's why the Academy offers detailed training on how to implement each of the five steps, along with tips and techniques for keeping consultations on track. We also offer our Members feedback and mentoring services, so they can become experts at initial consultations.

We've found that Members who take advantage of these services are those who experience the greatest reduction in stress and the greatest increase in retention rates. To top it off, these Members grow leaps and bounds in their ability to counsel their clients.

As your retention rates go up, so does the pressure to produce quality, error-free documents, and to do it quickly and efficiently.

What does the workflow process look like at your firm? If you're not quite ready to handle a large new caseload, you are not alone. Many firms do not have a reliable workflow process in place. Mistakes and misplaced information are common, leading to frustrated employees and unhappy clients.

KNOCK THEIR SOCKS OFF: HOW TO DRAFT, REVIEW, AND EXECUTE STATE-OF-THE-ART ESTATE PLANS

Has this ever happened to you?

You have a smooth, productive first consultation that ends with a new client retaining your firm. Now, it's time to get to work. You and the client choose a date for the final signing, and you forward your notes from the consultation to your office team.

Then, chaos ensues. Maybe your team doesn't include the correct forms in your client's file, or maybe they're inattentive to detail, forcing you to send the file back for correction after correction (or heaven forbid, you didn't fill out the Client Intake Form properly). Perhaps the documents aren't ready on time, forcing you to reschedule the signing, much to your client's frustration. Or maybe everything seems perfect until the client comes to your office for the final signing, only to spot a misspelled name or an incorrect address—forcing you to stop the signing and correct and reprint reams of documents.

In too many firms, the back office production of documents is a nightmare.

That is why the Academy developed a system for producing state-of-the-art documents in a reasonable amount of time, with very little stress in the office. The result is happy clients, happy employees, and a happy attorney.

The system allows you to track work from the moment your firm is retained, produce error-free documents, and create a surrounding rapport—a "wow" transformational experience—that will win you clients for life.

Our Efficient Workflow System has 12 steps:

PLANNING PHASE

Step One: You complete the client intake form, receive the retainer, and schedule the final signing at a time you know your staff can produce the documents.

Step Two: You take a few moments to proof the client intake form, making sure all names are spelled correctly and there is no missing information.

You then place the client's information (a client information form, the retainer check, and your firm's legal services agreement) into a color-coded packet. The Academy provides these folders to its Members so important information about a client's file is available at a glance.

- Green folders are for clients who are ready to go forward
- Yellow folders are for clients who have questions or special conditions that must be addressed
- Red folders are for rush jobs

Step Three: You forward the client's folder to your firm's data entry staff and they enter the client's data into your system.

Step Four: Your accounting staff gets the folder and the tracking form and makes the appropriate entries into your firm's accounting software. Then, the folder is forwarded to your document production staff.

DOCUMENT PRODUCTION PHASE

Step Five: Your data entry staff receives the folder, reviews all the information you received in the initial consultation, proofs your work on the client intake form for accuracy, and assembles, reviews, and prints the client's documents.

Step Six: Your data entry staff sends out the appropriate follow-up letter, requesting any necessary information and confirming the date and time of the final signing. This step saves phone calls from worried clients and lets them know they haven't been forgotten. Then, the client's folder, including the draft documents, is forwarded to your production proofing staff.

Step Seven: Your production proofing staff goes over the client's documents with a fine-toothed comb. Assisting in this process is the Academy's checklist. There is one version of the checklist for married clients, and a separate version for unmarried clients. If mistakes are spotted, the client's folder goes back to your data entry staff for correction. After the production proofing staff is confident the client's documents are error-free, the folder is sent to you.

Step Eight: You get the final printed documents and proof them, making sure the documents meet the client's needs and accurately reflect the information you gathered at the initial consultation. If you find mistakes, the folder goes back to your data entry staff so corrections can be made. Every step of the way, each addition and adjustment to your client's folder is entered into your database. This way, every detail of the client's interaction with your firm is tracked from the first moment.

Step Nine: The Academy recognizes that human error is a part of any process where people are involved. Rather than having clients come to your office for the final signing, only to spot an error that requires you to stop the signing process and fix the client's documents, we designed our Efficient Workflow Systems to include a phone final review. During this step in the process, your final signing paralegal receives the client's folder along with the Academy checklist. Then, he or she calls the client to verify the spelling of all names, check birthdates, and verify all the other details on the checklist. Then, your paralegal reconfirms the date and time of the final signing and reminds the client of the balance of fees due. The result is that there are no nasty surprises to derail the final signing.

Step Ten: After the final signing paralegal verifies that all the documents are error-free and ready for signing, the client's folder is forwarded to your portfolio assembly staff. This person assembles two sets of documents. The first set is to be signed by the client, and the second set is three-hole punched so it can be placed in the client's portfolio.

Step Eleven: Your staff assembles the appropriate funding documents, prints them, and places them in the client folder.

They then check to make sure all documents are in order for the final signing.

FOLLOW-UP

Step Twelve: This step applies when you have a client who procrastinates. Your final signing paralegal merges the appropriate letter to send to the procrastinating client, and changes the status of the file from active to inactive. This helps you avoid leaving the client's file in limbo and risking an unsatisfied client, not to mention potential penalties for an ethics violation.

THE FINAL SIGNING*

After all these steps are completed, it is time for the final signing. This part of the process is a mixture of art and science. At first, you will conduct the final signings for your clients. Eventually, however, the Academy encourages each firm to have at least one final signing paralegal, and to delegate the final signing to this person. Your final signing paralegal is one of your prime team members because they get a chance to deepen your relationship with each client.

 The Final Signing meeting is very important. Complete training is crucial. The Academy has a separate final signing system, which is explained in a special DVD training made available to Members.

The DVD features an expert final signing paralegal who walks the paralegal through all the steps involved. This ensures that each of your clients receives the very best care and attention at the final signing.

With this workflow system in place, your clients get flawless documents, well presented in a portfolio, all drafted and ready to sign within a reasonable amount of time. They also get to experience a well organized final signing with a professional who cares about their experience with your firm. All of this combines to provide your clients with a "wow" transformational experience—one that sets you apart from all the other law firms in your community and helps you win your clients' lifetime loyalty.

With a growing law firm and happy clients, it is time to shift your focus slightly and think about how you'll stay on top of your game as a legal technician.

We keep mentioning that the attorney needs to be driving the business and counselling clients. Staying on top of the law is a full time job and it is important to have personal confidence in what you are saying and what you're providing to clients in the form of your legal advice and documents.

> *The best way to ensure that you stay on the cutting edge of legal strategy, tools, and education is to have a dedicated system.*

Without a system in place or a source you trust, much of your revenue producing time may be spent in an area that should, in reality, be delegated to other team members.

STAYING AHEAD OF THE PACK

One of the ways you can best serve your clients is to be an excellent legal technician. Clients assume you'll continually stay on top of the latest in estate planning law and strategy, and will be able to implement cutting-edge strategies to meet their needs. **The areas of expertise you need to look for support in are:**

- Basic and advanced estate planning education and CLE
- The best legal strategies for specific client situations
- Current document language to execute each strategy
- Legal experts in estate, tax, trust, elder law, and entity planning for brainstorming, assistance in research or sources for co-counselling in areas not routinely practiced

As an example, the authors of the legal documents the Academy Members use are the same exact attorneys that Members consult with for strategies. The Legal Education Department keeps the documents updated, they review case facts with

Members and consult on additional planning ideas or point Members to the right place for study on services they may not routinely offer.

Having your left hand know what your right hand is doing, is key. If you use documents from one place, marketing from another, research from yet another source... sometimes they just aren't put together in the best way.

System 10: Ancillary Business

As the pieces fall into place and your firm begins to not only grow but to truly thrive, you may want to consider implementing our next system. With the Academy's Ancillary Business System, you have the opportunity to strategically add one or more businesses to your law firm.

If your law firm runs like a well-oiled machine, with all the necessary systems in place, it will grow. You'll polish your marketing strategy and perfect a system for conducting consultations, and you'll start to retain more clients. You'll implement systems so your back

The Entrepreneurial Lawyer → **87**

office work happens seamlessly and your firm produces top-notch, error-free documents within a reasonable amount of time. Word will get out that you offer your clients a transformational experience and a level of service they can't get from any other firm in town. This will lead to more new clients, as well as a lasting relationship with your existing clients and their families.

ADDING TO THE SERVICES YOU OFFER

Over the past 20+ years this is the pattern the Academy's Members have followed, and we believe that one way to add value to your clients' experiences with your firm is to strategically add one or more ancillary businesses to your practice. This turns your firm into a mini-conglomerate, a one-stop shop where your clients can get many of their needs met. In addition to reinforcing your position as an indispensable source of advice and help to your clients, it has some added benefits for you:

- Ethically operated, an ancillary business can be a tremendous source of additional value to the client and revenue to the firm.

- The services you offer through your ancillary business help set you apart from competitor law firms, enhancing your reputation in the community and bringing in more clients.

- The additional services you offer allow you to stop worrying about competing on price. it becomes impossible to engage in an apples-to-apples comparison between the services offered by your firm and the mere documents offered by other firms.

Academy firms have added a number of ancillary businesses to their practices, including:

FINANCIAL SERVICES

Where do your clients go for financial advice and help with wealth management? Many of our Members have added a financial services component to their firms so they can provide clients with a financial plan that dovetails with their estate plan. With appropriate disclosure in most states, there is no problem.

Clients like the idea that when they die, the estate they want to pass to the next generation... actually exists. The attorney being involved in helping them make sure that happens is reassuring. We've found that attorneys getting involved in Financial Services for the sheer purpose of "making more money" never find the success that the attorney committed to helping the client will find.

FUNERAL TRUSTS AND LEGACY SAFEGUARD

Have you ever talked to your clients about how they plan to pay for their funeral? Too many people have not given thought to this important component of end of life planning, and their families ultimately suffer when they're forced into last-minute funeral planning combined with scrambling to cover funeral expenses.

Many of our Members offer funeral trusts along with Legacy Safeguard memberships for their clients. The funeral trust allows insurance policy funds to be set aside and protected until the need arises to pay for a client's funeral, and Legacy Safeguard offers a number of benefits, including:

- Assistance with finding a funeral home, planning the funeral and negotiating the price of the funeral

- End of life planning, guidance, and assistance

- Support for survivors, including bereavement travel assistance and discounts, as well as a personal advisor to help with hotel and restaurant services and other needs

- Tools for celebrating life events and preserving a legacy of family memories, history, and other information for a client's children and grandchildren

 PLEASE NOTE: Academy Members enjoy access to and support in operating these and other ancillary businesses, but we advise against rushing to start an additional business.

Email Questions@aaepa.com and ask us to send you our 45-minute recorded interview on incorporating financial services into your firm.

We firmly believe that the systems in your law firm should be solid before you launch a second business. The timing of such a venture is critical, and it is imperative that you know which licenses to study for, how to handle the staffing and accounting for this business, and how to ensure that the separation of files meets requirements.

If you are interested in all the ways in which our Ancillary Business System can enrich your life and help you add immense value to your clients' experience with your firm, contact us at Questions@aaepa.com or give us a call at (800)846-1555. We'll be happy to discuss the details with you and put you in touch with Academy members who have launched thriving ancillary businesses.

The size of your department or law firm can make you feel isolated, especially when you do things differently than other attorneys in your area. This is where our final system comes in. it is specifically designed to combat this sense of isolation, give you a sense of community, and keep you on the cutting edge.

> *As a solo practitioner or the head of a small estate planning firm, it's difficult to stay on the cutting edge of developments in the law and innovative strategies for meeting your clients' needs, not to mention keeping up with the latest in law firm technology, marketing ideas, and other tools for managing your practice.*

If you look at some of the most successful business people in the news or in your community, you will find that they spend time with others just like them. Bill Gates hangs out with Warren Buffet. They socialize some, they chat, they debate, they study what the other is doing and they like each other.

It is not common that attorneys are able to connect with other attorneys doing the same type of thing they do and accomplish what Gates and Buffet accomplish.

Leading a small law firm can also be a lonely prospect. You don't have the benefit of a staff full of attorneys to collaborate with or bounce ideas off. Even if you're active in your local bar association, your colleagues are likely less than forthcoming when it comes to sharing details about how their firms actually operate, marketing secrets they've learned, or how their firm's finances are structured. You're left to learn how to grow your practice and better serve your clients by trial and error.

The "Mastermind" concept is as old as Napoleon Hill. It's common knowledge that this is a primary element of success, yet it is one of the most neglected things we tend to do.

Sometimes ego gets in the way, sometimes, it's just hard to get to know the right people.

One of the most unexpected, hard-to-describe things showed up when the Academy launched in 1993. Collegiality. The gathering of like-minded entrepreneurial attorneys has had a huge impact on attorneys across the country.

With some intention and effort you can create your own relationships that give you support, insights, offer you a place to mentor someone else. We understand that. In an effort to outline what you can look for in your professional mastermind groups, please read on about what the Academy has put in place. We feel that these ingredients have a lot to do with the depth of the relationship we see amongst our Members.

The Academy has addressed these challenges by not only providing the information and tools our Members need to operate cutting edge estate planning firms, but by helping our Members link to a nationwide network of like-minded attorneys. We have cultivated what our Members often refer to as a family atmosphere. Chances are, interacting with Academy attorneys is unlike any experience you've had with other attorneys. Not only do our Members have a sense of camaraderie with each other, they're eager to share ideas and insights with each other.

GEOGRAPHIC TERRITORIES

One of the reasons for this uniquely collegial environment is that we make sure our Members don't have to compete with each other for clients. When a new Member joins the Academy, he or she signs a Membership agreement. Among other things, this agreement ensures that Academy marketing materials, documents, and other benefits are not available to just anyone. The Academy only admits a limited number of firms in any given geographic territory. We determine our territories by population, media support, and geography. We also consider the location of the Member's existing client base.

Academy Members are not competitors, so they are free to ask questions, share information and ideas, and interact with each other as trusted colleagues. And because our Members share the entrepreneurial spirit, they're on the same page with regard to goals for their firms. This means the information they offer each other is practical, applicable, and genuine.

EVENTS

Each year, the Academy holds two Summits; one in the Spring and one in the Fall. Summits are an opportunity for our Members to break free of their routines and come together for:

- Training and instruction on marketing and practice management
- In-depth legal education sessions
- Social activities

Summits allow Members to refresh their knowledge of Academy systems and tools, get the latest updates on marketing, practice management, and legal strategies, and spend time with other Members face-to-face.

LISTSERV

The Academy operates a Members-Only Listserv, and many of our Members rely on this resource because it provides a continuous, active exchange of ideas about the practice of estate planning law. Most of the discussions on the listserv focus on technical legal matters, so it can be an excellent resource for staying abreast of the latest ideas and information.

OTHER OPPORTUNITIES

Members have a variety of other opportunities to interact with each other and share ideas. For example, the Academy holds frequent webinars, as well as live Classroom Conference Calls. These events, produced by our education department, help Members keep tabs on the latest in legal thinking and strategies. They also make Members aware of the issues faced by their colleagues around the country—and the often innovative ways those issues are being addressed.

We also maintain a Member sharing area on the Academy's website. This area contains an online clause bank where Members can share sample language that has helped them draft documents to meet their clients' needs. It also contains a variety of other Member-submitted ideas and innovations. For instance, Members use this portion of our website to share materials for seminars they've presented, successful practice management strategies and internal office policies, and letters they've sent to clients.

If you would like to know more about what it's like to participate in the Academy's community of attorneys, contact us at Questions@aaepa.com or give us a call at (800) 846-1555. We'll put you in touch with Members who are happy to share their experiences.

Since 1993, the American Academy of Estate Planning Attorneys has coached hundreds of attorneys from all over the United States as they transformed their practices into thriving and important business enterprises.

Academy Members have access to an entire range of support and benefits. For example, new Members receive assistance in assessing their current practice and envisioning their ideal firm, down to the last detail.

They're also given access to—and help in implementing—the 11 Essential Systems you've just read about as well as working one-on-one with a Practice Building Consultant to implement the systems, set short- and long-term goals, and remain accountable for achieving them. Members have access to cutting-edge technology; a responsive legal education department staffed with top legal minds; and a nationwide network of colleagues, many of whom are at the forefront of their field.

And this is just the beginning. The Academy is committed to giving its Members the support they need to offer unparalleled services to their clients.